Opposites!

HARD AND SOFT

BY EMILIE DUFRESNE

BookLife PUBLISHING

©2018
Book Life
King's Lynn
Norfolk PE30 4LS

ISBN: 978-1-78637-417-2

All rights reserved
Printed in Malaysia

Written by:
Emilie Dufresne

Edited by:
Kirsty Holmes

Designed by:
Jasmine Pointer

A catalogue record for this book is available from the British Library.

All facts, statistics, web addresses and URLs in this book were verified as valid and accurate at time of writing. No responsibility for any changes to external websites or references can be accepted by either the author or publisher.

OXFORDSHIRE LIBRARY SERVICE	
3303448814	
Askews & Holts	19-Nov-2018
P428.1	£12.99

CONTENTS

Page 4	What Are Opposites?
Page 6	Sweets
Page 8	Materials
Page 10	Land Animals
Page 12	Clothing
Page 14	Toys
Page 16	Sea Creatures
Page 18	Liquids
Page 20	Activity
Page 22	Answers
Page 24	Glossary and Index

Words that look like **this** can be found in the glossary on page 24.

WHAT ARE OPPOSITES?

An opposite is when two things are completely different.

SOME EXAMPLES OF OPPOSITES ARE…

HARD AND SOFT

WET AND DRY

LIGHT AND DARK

LOUD AND quiet

HOT AND COLD

BIG AND small

Something that is **HARD** is not the same as something that is SOFT.

HARD AND SOFT ARE OPPOSITES.

SWEETS

Some sweets are hard. Rock is a hard sweet. It is usually mint flavoured.

Marshmallows are soft and squidgy. You can put them on top of hot chocolates!

ROCK AND MARSHMALLOWS ARE OPPOSITES!

MATERIALS

Bricks are made from a material that is hard. Bricks have to be strong enough to build houses.

BRICKS AND PILLOWS ARE OPPOSITES.

Pillows are soft. They are made out of soft materials like feathers and cotton.

LAND ANIMALS

Armadillos have a hard shell on the outside of their bodies. Their shells help protect them.

MANY ARMADILLOS CAN ROLL INTO A BALL SHAPE.

ARMADILLOS AND CHINCHILLAS ARE OPPOSITES.

Chinchillas have some of the softest hair in the world. 50 hairs can grow from each **follicle**!

CLOTHING

These are hard hats. They keep your head safe from falling objects.

HARD HATS AND JUMPERS ARE OPPOSITES.

Jumpers are often made of soft fabrics. This makes them snuggly and warm to wear.

TOYS

Remote-control cars are hard. They are made out of plastic so they don't break easily.

REMOTE-CONTROL CARS AND SLIME ARE OPPOSITES.

Slime is soft. You can **mould** it into different shapes and pull it in all different directions!

SEA CREATURES

Giant spider crabs have hard shells.

GIANT SPIDER CRABS CAN LIVE FOR UP TO 100 YEARS!

GIANT SPIDER CRABS AND JELLYFISH ARE OPPOSITES.

Jellyfish are soft. They have no bones in their bodies! Watch out... their tentacles can sting!

LIQUIDS

When some liquids **freeze** they become **solid**. When water freezes it becomes ice. Ice is hard.

When solids melt, they turn back into liquids.
When ice melts, it becomes water. Water is soft.

ICE AND WATER ARE OPPOSITES.

ACTIVITY

Which of these things are **HARD**, and which are SOFT?

SLIME

ARMADILLO

REMOTE-CONTROL CAR

ANSWERS

ROCK

ARMADILLO

REMOTE-CONTROL CAR

That's right! These ones are **HARD**!

These ones are SOFT!

MARSHMALLOWS

CHINCHILLA

SLIME

23

GLOSSARY

follicle — small sacs in the body that surround things, like hair and nails

freeze — when something gets so cold it becomes hard

mould — to form a shape out of a flexible material

solid — a firm and stable substance, not a liquid

INDEX

animals 10–11, 16–17
hot chocolate 7
houses 8
marshmallows 7
sea 16–17
water 18–19

Photocredits:
Images are courtesy of Shutterstock.com. With thanks to Getty Images, Thinkstock Photo and iStockphoto.
Front cover - Kimberly Hall, wimammoth, Atesevich, pterwort, FabrikaSimf, Dima Moroz, Susan Schmitz, MO_SES Premium, DenisNata, Jiri Hera, Africa Studio, Christopher Hall, SeDmi, AVN Photo Lab, ROLAND ANCLA LEGASPI, Luccia, azure1, Mega Pixel, alexandarilich, Pixfiction, JIANG HONGYAN. 2 - Pongsatorn Singnoy. 3 - DenisNata. 4 - Lopolo. 5 – owlpro, Maciej Czekajewski. 6 – sirtravelalot. 7 – Gita Kulinitch Studio, iiian Oksana. 8 - Ewelina Wachala. 9 - Syda Productions. 10 - Vladimir Wrangel. 11 - Africa Studio. 12 - DutchScenery. 13 - ESB Professional. 14 – intararit. 15 - jarabee123. 16 - Lerner Vadim. 17 - H.Tanaka. 18 - Volodymyr Krasyuk. 19 – robert_s. 20 – jarabee123, Vladimir Wrangel, intararit. 21 – Gita Kulinitch Studio, Africa Studio, sirtravelalot. 22 – sirtravelalot, Vladimir Wrange, intararit. 23 – Gita Kulinitch Studio, Africa Studio. 23 - jarabee123. 24 - azure1.